CHI

02-06

FRIENDS
OF ACPL

SandCastle

Word Families Set 1

-at as in cat

Mary Elizabeth Salzmann

Consulting Editor Monica Marx, M.A./Reading Specialist

ABDO
Publishing Company

Published by SandCastle™, an imprint of ABDO Publishing Company, 4940 Viking Drive, Edina, Minnesota 55435.

Printed in the United States.

Credits
Edited by: Pam Price
Curriculum Coordinator: Nancy Tuminelly
Cover and Interior Design and Production: Mighty Media
Photo Credits: Brand X Pictures, Comstock, Corbis Images, Eyewire Images, Hemera, PhotoDisc

Library of Congress Cataloging-in-Publication Data

Salzmann, Mary Elizabeth, 1968-
         -At as in cat / Mary Elizabeth Salzmann.
            p. cm. -- (Word families. Set I)
         Summary: Introduces, in brief text and illustrations, the use of the letter combination "at" in such words as "cat," "hat," "flat," and "that."
         ISBN 1-59197-221-3
         1. Readers (Primary) [1. Vocabulary. 2. Reading.] I. Title.

    PE1119 .S2342148 2003
    428.1--dc21   2002038622

SandCastle™ books are created by a professional team of educators, reading specialists, and content developers around five essential components that include phonemic awareness, phonics, vocabulary, text comprehension, and fluency. All books are written, reviewed, and leveled for guided reading, early intervention reading, and Accelerated Reader® programs and designed for use in shared, guided, and independent reading and writing activities to support a balanced approach to literacy instruction.

Let Us Know

After reading the book, SandCastle would like you to tell us your stories about reading. What is your favorite page? Was there something hard that you needed help with? Share the ups and downs of learning to read. We want to hear from you! To get posted on the ABDO Publishing Company Web site, send us e-mail at:

sandcastle@abdopub.com

SandCastle Level: Transitional

-at Words

bat

cat

hat

mat

rat

vat

Ned is ready to swing the bat.

Deb plays with her cat.

Wendy wears a white
hat.

The plate sits on a mat.

Peg has a pet rat.

The black cat sits next
to a vat.

Pitter-Pat
the Cat

Nat has a pet cat
named Pitter-Pat.

Nat gave Pitter-Pat
a plastic bat.

Pitter-Pat played
with the bat
on a mat.

Pitter-Pat played
with the bat
under a big hat.

Pitter-Pat played with the
bat inside a vat.

Then Nat gave Pitter-Pat
a toy rat.

Pitter-Pat played with the rat inside the vat.

Pitter-Pat played
with the rat
under the big hat.

Pitter-Pat played
with the rat
on the mat.

After all that, Pitter-Pat
was tired, so she sat!

Pitter-Pat sat on Nat!

Nat said, "Pitter-Pat,
you're a silly cat!"

The -at Word Family

bat	Nat
cat	Pitter-Pat
chat	rat
fat	sat
flat	slat
hat	that
mat	vat

Glossary

Some of the words in this list may have more than one meaning. The meaning listed here reflects the way the word is used in the book.

bat   a wooden or metal stick used to hit a ball; a small flying animal that sleeps during the day and comes out at night

plastic   a man-made material that is light and strong and can be made into different shapes

vat   a large container used to hold liquids

About SandCastle™

A professional team of educators, reading specialists, and content developers created the SandCastle™ series to support young readers as they develop reading skills and strategies and increase their general knowledge. The SandCastle™ series has four levels that correspond to early literacy development in young children. The levels are provided to help teachers and parents select the appropriate books for young readers.

Emerging Readers
(no flags)

Beginning Readers
(1 flag)

Transitional Readers
(2 flags)

Fluent Readers
(3 flags)

These levels are meant only as a guide. All levels are subject to change.

To see a complete list of SandCastle™ books and other nonfiction titles from ABDO Publishing Company, visit **www.abdopub.com** or contact us at:

4940 Viking Drive, Edina, Minnesota 55435 • 1-800-800-1312 • fax: 1-952-831-1632